ANCIENT MESOPOTAMIA

ANCIENT CIVILIZATIONS IN REVIEW

By Seth Lynch

Enslow Publishing

Please visit our website, www.enslow.com. For a free color catalog of all our high-quality books, call toll free 1-800-398-2504 or fax 1-877-980-4454.

Library of Congress Cataloging-in-Publication Data
Names: Lynch, Seth, author.
Title: Ancient Mesopotamia / Seth Lynch.
Description: Buffalo, New York : Enslow Publishing, [2025] | Series: Ancient civilizations in review | Includes bibliographical references and index.
Identifiers: LCCN 2024023839 | ISBN 9781978542792 (library binding) | ISBN 9781978542785 (paperback) | ISBN 9781978542808 (ebook)
Subjects: LCSH: Iraq–Civilization–To 634–Juvenile literature.
Classification: LCC DS70.62 .L96 2025 | DDC 935–dc23/eng/20240605
LC record available at https://lccn.loc.gov/2024023839

Published in 2025 by
Enslow Publishing
2544 Clinton Street
Buffalo, NY 14224

Portions of this work were originally authored by Daniel R. Faust and published as *Ancient Mesopotamia*. All new material this edition authored by Seth Lynch.

Designer: Leslie Taylor
Editor: Kristen Nelson

Photo credits: Cover (city ruins) syekteese/Shutterstock, (tablet) Gokhan Dogan/Shutterstock.com, (vase) Arda_ALTAY/Shutterstock.com; (back cover) FrentaN/Shutterstock.com; Cover and series art (vintage map) Andrey_Kuzmin/Shutterstock.com (brush strokes) ozzichka/Shutterstock.com, (font) MagicPics/Shutterstock.com; p. 5 CHAOSPHERE/Shutterstock.com; p. 7 Fedor Selivanov/Shutterstock.com; p. 8 Anonymous/File:Ur chariot.jpg_commons.wikimedia.org; p. 9 Sergeyziegler/File:Sumerian planisphere.jpg_commons.wikimedia.org; p. 10 Kamira/Shutterstock.com; p. 11 Gokhan Dogan/Shutterstock.com; p. 12 The British Museum Collections/File:Ea (Babilonian) - EnKi (Sumerian).jpg_wikimedia.org; p. 13 (top) Mohammed_Al_Ali/Shutterstock.com, (bottom) mohannad mohannad/Shutterstock.com; p. 15 matrioshka/Shutterstock.com; p. 17 1882: excavated by Hormuzd Rassam. Place: Sippar./ile:Votive monument to Hammurabi BM 22454 n01.jpg_wikimedia.org; p. 19 Hammurabi (–1810—1750) anonymous/File:F0182 Louvre Code Hammourabi Bas-relief Sb8 rwk.jpg_wikimedia.org; p. 21 (top) Prisma Archivo/Alamy.com, (bottom) FrentaN/Shutterstock.com; p. 23 ArtMediaFactory/Shutterstock.com; p. 25 AstralManSigmaDelta/Shutterstock.com; p. 27 Mistervlad/Shutterstock.com; p. 29 Mahmoud Suhail/Shutterstock.com.

Printed in the United States of America

CPSIA compliance information: Batch #CWENS25: For further information, contact Enslow Publishing at 1-800-398-2504.

CONTENTS

Words in the glossary appear in **bold** the first time they are used in the text.

First Civilization

More than 6,500 years ago, one of the first **civilizations** rose in **ancient** Mesopotamia. Mesopotamia was part of the "Fertile Crescent." This was a crescent, or moon-shaped, area of land that was fertile, or great for growing crops.

LEARN MORE

Mesopotamia means "country between two rivers" in Greek. Ancient people settled there between the Tigris and Euphrates Rivers in present-day Iraq and Kuwait.

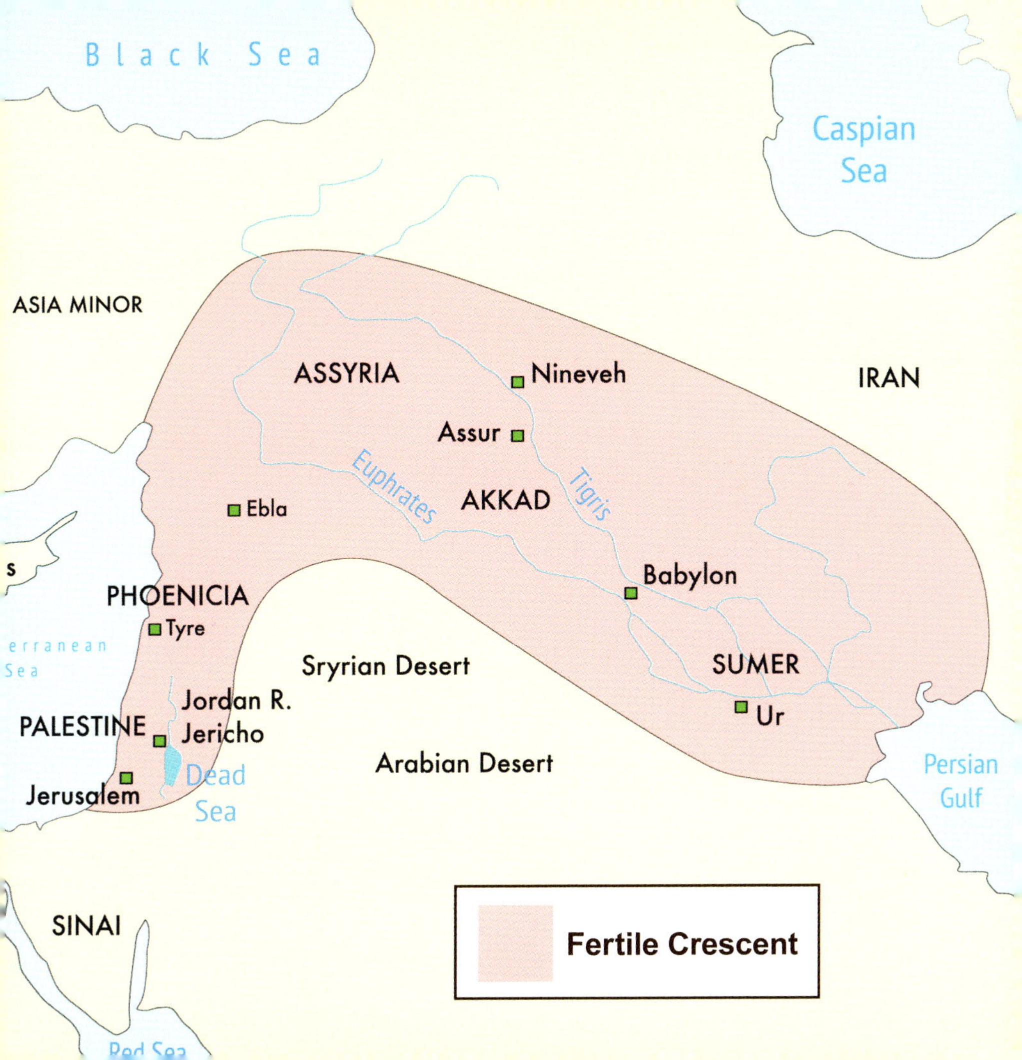

Black Sea
Caspian Sea
ASIA MINOR
ASSYRIA
Nineveh
IRAN
Assur
Euphrates
Tigris
AKKAD
Ebla
s
Babylon
PHOENICIA
Tyre
erranean Sea
Sryrian Desert
SUMER
Jordan R.
Jericho
PALESTINE
Ur
Dead Sea
Jerusalem
Arabian Desert
Persian Gulf
SINAI
Fertile Crescent

The Sumerians

Farming began in ancient Mesopotamia around 10,000 BCE or earlier. Farming settlements grew into the Sumerian civilization. The Sumerians built irrigation systems, which were ways to bring water to their crops. As Sumerian villages grew into cities, they set up a government.

LEARN MORE

Kish, Lagash, Uruk, and Ur were some of the big cities in Sumer.

The Sumerian civilization invented the wheel! Around 3500 BCE, they began to use wheels to make **pottery**. Later, they used the wheel to make **vehicles**. The Sumerians also built ships. They sailed down the Tigris and Euphrates Rivers to the Persian Gulf.

LEARN MORE

The Sumerians also inventted an early calendar. It was based on the **phases** of the moon.

ancient Sumerian star chart

The Sumerians used their ships to trade with other early civilizations, such as those in the north of India. They traded cloth, tools, and more. The Sumerians invented writing called cuneiform to keep track of their traded goods.

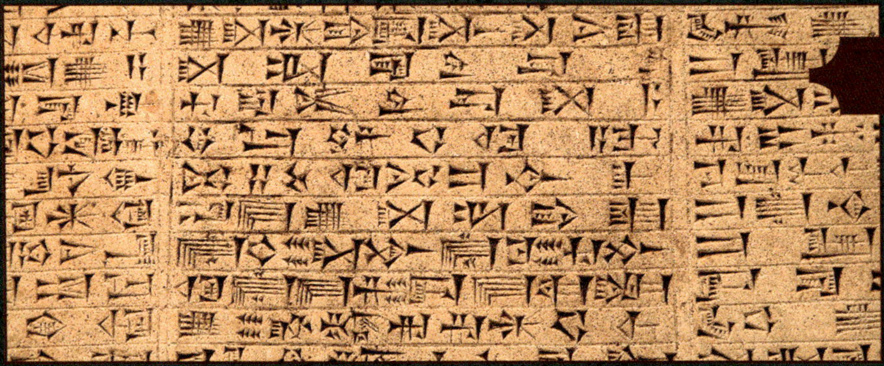

LEARN MORE

Cuneiform used about 600 **wedge**-shaped **symbols**. These symbols were pressed into tablets, or flat pieces, of soft clay.

cuneiform

The Sumerian people built their cities with a ziggurat at the center. Many ziggurats had a stepped **pyramid** shape. These buildings honored a god and raised **priests** and priestesses closer to the heavens. **City-states** formed around the cities. Each city-state ruled itself.

Sumerian gods

LEARN MORE

The Sumerians believed in thousands of gods.

ziggurat at Ur

The First Empire

Akkad, a city-state north of Sumer, took over the Sumerians around 2350 BCE. The Akkadian Empire was likely the world's first empire. It built roads to connect, or join, its cities and set up the first ways to send mail.

LEARN MORE

An empire is many countries or peoples that are under the control of one ruler or government.

Babylon Rises

The Akkadian Empire fell around 2150 BCE after less than 200 years in power. A group called the Amorites conquered Mesopotamia around 1900 BCE. The new empire became known as Babylonia after the city of Babylon, its capital, or main city.

LEARN MORE

Starting in 1792 BCE, King Hammurabi ruled Babylonia. He grew the Babylonian Empire by conquering, or taking over, land in northern and southern Mesopotamia.

Hammurabi

The Code of Hammurabi

Hammurabi wrote laws called the Code of Hammurabi. The code was made up of 282 laws all people in the empire had to follow. However, there were different laws for men and women. Poor people faced worse **punishments** for breaking the law than rich people too.

LEARN MORE

The saying "an eye for an eye" comes from the Code of Hammurabi.

Assyrian Army

The Babylonians began to lose power around 1600 BCE. The Assyrians of northern Mesopotamia began to build their empire in the 1300s BCE. They had a strong army. It used iron **weapons**, which were better than other weapons of the time.

LEARN MORE

The Assyrian Empire's army was one of the first to use chariots. Chariots are two-wheeled wagons pulled by horses.

chariot

Assyrian fighters

The Assyrian Empire conquered Mesopotamia, much of the Middle East, and as far as Egypt by 671 BCE. The empire became too large to govern however. Babylonians, also called Chaldeans, worked with other groups to take down the weakening empire. The Assyrian Empire fell in 609 BCE.

LEARN MORE

One of the last Assyrian kings built a library in the Assyrian city of Nineveh. It held thousands of cuneiform tablets of Sumerian and Babylonian letters, histories, and more.

cuneiform
tablets from the
library in Ninevah

Rebuilding Babylon

The Chaldean Empire is sometimes also called the New Babylonian Empire. One of its kings, Nebuchadnezzar II, rebuilt the city of Babylon and made it the capital of the new empire. It didn't last long. In 539 BCE, the Persian Empire conquered Babylon.

LEARN MORE

Nebuchadnezzar II built a palace in Babylon. It may have been home to the Hanging Gardens of Babylon. No one knows for sure if this ancient wonder was a real garden or just a story!

artist's idea of the Hanging Gardens of Babylon

Two Empires

The Persian (or Achaemenid) Empire grew to be one of the largest empires ever. In the 330s BCE, Alexander the Great conquered the Persian Empire. He took control of Mesopotamia, as well as Egypt and land around the Mediterranean Sea.

LEARN MORE

Alexander the Great's empire began around present-day Greece. At its largest, it controlled land into northwestern India.

Alexander the Great

The Loss of Mesopotamia

Ancient Mesopotamia continued to be ruled by outsiders into the next century and beyond. Much of the Mesopotamian culture—or ideas, beliefs, and ways of life—were lost. The great cities of this civilization did not last until the present either.

LEARN MORE

The ruins of Nebuchadnezzar II's Babylon can be found about 60 miles (100 km) from Baghdad, Iraq, today.

Babylonian ruins

Timeline of Ancient Mesopotamia

c. 10,000 BCE .... Farming begins in Mesopotamia.

c. 4000 BCE .... The Sumerian civilization rises.

c. 3500 BCE .... The Sumerians invent the wheel.

c. 2350 BCE .... The Akkadians conquer the Sumerians. The Akkadian Empire rises.

c. 2150 BCE .... The Akkadian Empire falls.

c. 1900 BCE.... The Babylonian Empire rises.

1792 BCE .... Hammurabi becomes king of Babylon.

1300s BCE ..... The Assyrians rise to power.

609 BCE .... The Assyrian Empire falls to the Babylonians and others.

539 BCE .... The Persian Empire conquers Babylon.

330s BCE .... Alexander the Great conquers the Persian Empire.

GLOSSARY

ancient: Very old or having to do with the past long ago.

city-state: A government in which an independent city rules over the surrounding area as well as itself.

civilization: Organized society with written records and laws.

phase: A stage in a process or sequence of events.

pottery: Bowls, plates, and art that are made by hand out of clay baked to become hard.

priest: A man who performs religious ceremonies. A priestess is a woman who performs religious ceremonies.

punishment: The act of making someone suffer or pay when they break a rule or law.

pyramid: A 3D shape that has a rectangular base and triangular sides.

symbol: A picture, shape, or object that stands for something else.

vehicle: An object that moves people and goods from one place to another.

weapon: Something used to fight an enemy.

wedge: Something that is shaped like a triangle.

FOR MORE INFORMATION

BOOKS

Faust, Daniel R. *The Rise and Fall of Mesopotamia.* Minneapolis, MN: Bearport Publishing Company, 2025.

Simons, Lisa M. Bolt. *Super Surprising Trivia About Ancient Civilizations.* North Mankato, MN: Capstone Press, 2024.

WEBSITE

Ducksters: Ancient Mesopotamia
https://www.ducksters.com/history/mesopotamia/ancient_mesopotamia.php
Read even more about ancient Mesopotamia here.

INDEX